DANGEROUS DINOSAURS

FLYING MONSTERS

Liz Miles

W
FRANKLIN WATTS
LONDON·SYDNEY

First published in 2015 by Franklin Watts

Copyright © Arcturus Holdings Limited

Franklin Watts
338 Euston Road
London
NW1 3BH

Franklin Watts Australia
Level 17/207 Kent Street, Sydney, NSW 2000

Produced by Arcturus Publishing Limited,
26/27 Bickels Yard, 151–153 Bermondsey Street, London SE1 3HA

The right of Liz Miles to be identified as the author of this work has
been asserted by her in accordance with the Copyright, Designs and
Patents Act 1988.

Author: Liz Miles
Editors: Joe Harris, Alex Woolf and Joe Fullman
Designer: Emma Randall
Original design concept: Notion Design

Picture Credits:
Key: b-bottom, m-middle, l-left, r-right, t-top
All images by pixel-shack.com except for:
Shutterstock: p9 b, p 14 b, p24 t, p24 b, p25 t, p24 r, p24 b.
Wikipedia Commons: p7 b, p21 t, p23 b.

A CIP catalogue record for this book is available from the British Library.

Dewey Decimal Classification Number: 567.9'18-dc23
ISBN: 978 1 4451 4160 2

Printed in China

Franklin Watts is a division of Hachette Children's Books, an Hachette
UK company.
www.hachette.co.uk

SL004434UK

Supplier 03, Date 1214, Print Run 3760

CONTENTS

SAVAGE SKIES

While the dinosaurs ruled the land, the pterosaurs (TEH-roe-sores) were the tyrants of the sky. These powerful reptiles flew over the sea, coasts and sometimes inland, snapping up insects, grabbing live fish or tearing at carrion.

Some had strong, toothless beaks, while others had needle-sharp teeth. They appeared around 200 million years ago and were at their peak in late Jurassic times, ranging from the size of tiny birds to monsters as big as a light aircraft. Swooping and gliding, pterosaurs could dive for fish in the sea or soar above the land, safe from the hungry jaws of the dinosaurs. Pterosaurs are traditionally divided into two types – pterodactyls (TEH-roe-DACK-tills) and rhamphorhynchoids (ram-foe-RINK-oids).

Winged pterosaurs soar above the Jurassic coast, out of reach of the dinosaurs below.

WINGED WONDERS

Pterosaur means 'winged lizard'. Each wing of these reptiles was made of a leathery, elastic membrane, or skin. The membrane stretched from the body across to a super-long fourth finger. The other fingers were clawed. The wing was thin but strong for flying, and did not tear easily.

NEEDLE-TOOTHED TERRORS

Rhamphorhynchus (ram-foe-RINK-us) had long fangs, a pointed beak and a 1.8-m (6-ft) wide wingspan for stability – perfect for a fish hunter. With its wide wings it could fly low over the sea or lakes, using its sharp eyes to seek food.

FISH BASKET

There may have been a pouch in Rhamphorhynchus's throat, like a pelican's, so that it could catch several fish in one go.

DIAMOND RUDDER

The long tail had a diamond-shaped flap at the end, which probably helped steer it through the air, like a boat's rudder.

BEAK SNOUT

Rhamphorhynchus means 'beak snout'. Its protruding beak held 34 needle-sharp teeth (ten pairs at the top and seven below). They stuck out to the side and at the front – like a spiked cage that even slippery fish could not escape.

Rhamphorhynchus probably hunted by swooping low over the surface of water, dipping in its toothy beak and snatching up prey. Some scientists think it may have caught several fish at once using a skimming technique – dragging its open beak along like an underwater plough. Its name gives away which of the two groups of pterosaurs it belongs to: it's a rhamphorhynchoid, not a pterodactyl. Rhamphorhynchoids had longer tails than pterodactyls.

Fang Face

Eudimorphodon (YOU-die-MORE-fo-don), another rhamphorhynchoid, had more than 100 teeth, and some of its teeth had more than one point. This mass of sharp teeth was deadly for any fish it caught, and allowed no escape. Its long, curled toe-claws could grasp onto trees or cliff-tops. From these lookout places it could easily take off. Eudimorphodon is one of the earliest pterosaurs.

FLYING MONSTER DETECTIVES

How do we know what pterosaurs ate? The type of teeth are a clue, but the best evidence is the creatures' fossilised stomach contents, such as the fish scales found in the stomach of a Eudimorphodon.

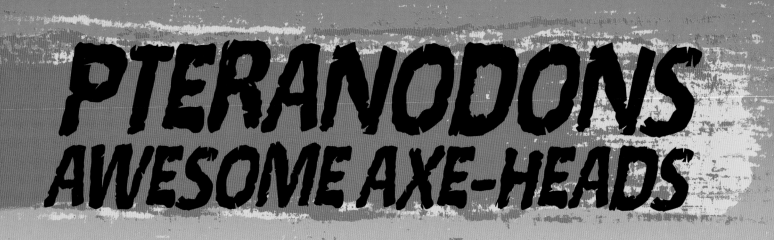

PTERANODONS
AWESOME AXE-HEADS

With a wingspan three times bigger than a golden eagle, and a pointed head longer than its own body, Pteranodon (teh-RAN-oh-don) was an awesome pterosaur. These monsters probably soared over coastlines, diving to snap up fish, squid and other Late Cretaceous creatures from the sea.

Although its jaws were toothless, they were powerful. Some Pteranodons had a large, backward-pointing head crest, giving them an aggressive, pickaxe-shaped profile. Like all pterodactyls, Pteranodon lacked a long tail, so the crest may have acted as a rudder, helping it to turn as it swooped through the sky.

SHOW-OFFS

Pteranodon is famous for its crest. Fossils show that the crests varied in size, and some were quite small. This suggests that rather than helping with flight, they may have been used by the males to attract mates. If that is the case, then it's likely that the crests were brightly patterned.

BEASTLY BEAK

Pteranodon's beak was 1.2 m (4 ft) in length – longer than its own body. Its shape allowed it to dip down deep, catch fish and swallow them whole.

LAUNCHED INTO THE AIR

On the shore, Pteranodon would have moved awkwardly on all fours. Some scientists believe that Pteranodons would have launched themselves into the air from high rocks. Others believe they could have landed on and taken off from the surface of the water, like modern-day gulls.

MICROLIGHT

Its wings were as wide as a microlight aircraft's, strengthened with gristle and supported by bone. With wings this size, Pteranodon would have flown without much flapping. In spite of its size, the monster could have moved quickly to snatch fish with ease.

THEN AND NOW

In the movie *Jurassic Park III*, Pteranodons are shown carrying people off in their claws. Could they really have lifted something as large as a human? After examining fossilised Pteranodon bones and working out what muscle power they had, it's clear that they would not have been strong enough to do this. But they could have carried a large fish, just a like a modern eagle.

JUTTING-JAWED
PTEROSAURS

Pterosaurs' fearsome jaws came in all sorts of weird shapes. Some creatures, like the Cearadactylus (see-AH-rah-DACK-till-us), had jaws similar to a crocodile's, while the jaws of Pterodaustro (TEH-roe-DAW-stroh) worked like those of a modern-day flamingo.

Other pterosaurs had spoonlike, upturned or crested jaws. Pterosaurs adapted to make the best of their environments and to get the food they needed to survive. Their jaws were specially shaped to capture and eat fish, shellfish, insects or carrion – so they had the perfect tools for crushing, sieving and biting.

NO ESCAPE

At the end of Cearadactylus's crocodile-like jaws was a semicircle of interlocking needle-like teeth. Once caught, no fish could escape this deadly trap. The remaining teeth were small and less sharp. This suggests that it didn't bother with chewing and probably ate its catch whole.

TWEEZER-TIGHT

The jaw of the Dsungaripterus (SUNG-ah-RIP-ter-us) had an upturned tip, which could have been used to lever clinging shellfish from rocks. Further back along the jaw there were bony, knob-like teeth. With the jaws shut tight, like tweezers or pliers, the knobs would have crushed the living prey from their shells.

A MEAN-LOOKING FLAMINGO?

The long, curved jaws of a Pterodaustro suggest that this pterosaur was a filter feeder, like a flamingo. Lowering its head to the water, it would scoop up surface water into its mouth. Anything living in the water would get stuck in the mass of 500 or so bristles in the lower jaw. Lots of little blunt teeth in the top jaw then brushed the food from between the bristles down its throat. Flamingos take their pink colour from the shrimps that they eat. Might Pterodaustro have been pink too?

PTERODAUSTRO VS FLAMINGO

	PTERODAUSTRO	FLAMINGO
BODY COVERING	Fur	Feathers
LENGTH	130 cm / 4 ft	106 cm / 42 in
WINGSPAN	3 m / 9.8 ft	1 m / 3 ft
WEIGHT	2-4.5 kg / 4.4-10 lb	2-4 kg / 4.4-8.8 lb

DIMORPHODON

TOOTH-BEAKED HUNTER

Dimorphodon (die-MORE-foe-don) was a fearsome fish- and insect-hunter. Its head was unusually big because of its deep jaws and mass of pointed teeth, which were ideal for impaling fish and carrying them off. It probably lived on cliffs or up trees, flying off to hunt for food and keeping away from predator dinosaurs.

BIG BITES
The deep beak allowed for large bites and big catches of fish. Such a big beak also made it easier to catch insects while flying. It may have been patterned for display, like a puffin's or a toucan's, perhaps showing off its presence during the breeding season.

FLAPPING FOR FISH
Dimorphodon wings were not as wide as some pterosaurs', so it may have needed to flap harder and faster to skim the seas.

CLINGING CLAWS
Dimorphodon had grasping claws on both its hands and its feet so that it could cling safely to tree trunks or the narrow ledges of sea cliffs.

LIGHT FOR FLIGHT

Dimorphodon's skull was large, but it contained empty spaces to make it light for flight. Although deep, its beak was narrow and streamlined so that it could cut through the air. If it rested on land, it probably crawled along on its two strong legs and wings. To take off, the wings were used for leverage – just as a pole-vaulter uses a pole to leap high.

MOUTH SPEARS

Dimorphodon's beak housed deadly weaponry. Its name means 'two-form teeth' and this is because it possessed two types of teeth: the sides of its jaws were lined with up to 40 small, sharp teeth, and there were two larger, piercing teeth at the front.

DIMORPHODON VERSUS PUFFIN

	DIMORPHODON	PUFFIN
LENGTH	1 m / 3.3 ft	25 cm / 10 in
WINGSPAN	1.2-1.8 cm / 4-6 ft	47- 63 cm / 19-25 in
WEIGHT	2267 g /5 lb	500 g / 17.5 oz
FLIGHT SPEED	Unknown	88 kph / 55 mph
FEET	Clawed	Webbed

FURRY FIENDS

Rhamphorhynchoids were warm-blooded and probably furry, which makes them sound almost cute. But they certainly weren't cute from the point of view of the fish, insects or other creatures they hunted.

As more types of rhamphorhynchoids appeared, their hunting and feeding tactics became more varied. Strange adaptations made them look like monsters, and scientists have looked for explanations for their bizarre body features.

KILLER TEETH

Jeholopterus (JAY-hole-OP-ter-us) was about the size of a house cat, with a 1-m (3-ft) wingspan. It had long, strong fangs in its top jaw, much larger than the rest of its teeth – like the fangs of a rattlesnake. Jeholopterus's claws were also sharper and larger than most other pterosaurs. Its jaws were built to open wide to snatch at insects in flight.

THEN AND NOW

Could Jeholopterus have been a bloodsucker, like a modern vampire bat? Some scientists have suggested that it may have used its long fangs to pierce the thick skin of dinosaurs and suck their blood. They say that it would have used its sharp claws to cling to the skin of the dinosaur while it attacked. However, there is little evidence to support this theory.

HAIRY HORROR

Even the name of this rhamphorhynchoid, Sordes (SORE-dess), is creepy. Sordes means 'filth' and is a reference to evil spirits in folk tales. It was named for its strange fur-like covering. Apart from a naked tail and wings, tiny hairs covered the whole of the creature's body. This led scientists to conclude that pterosaurs weren't cold-blooded killers at all – they were warm-blooded, like birds! As well as helping to keep them warm, a fur covering worked as a silencer, reducing the sound of its body in flight, so it could more easily take its prey by surprise.

QUETZALCOATLUS

GIANT VULTURE

Both terrifying and majestic, Quetzalcoatlus (KWET-zal-co-AT-lus) soared through the Late Cretaceous skies. With a wingspan of 11 m (36 ft), it is the biggest flying creature known to have lived, and a giant compared with the biggest bird (the wandering albatross). For food, it may have plucked fish from the sea, torn at carrion or probed in shallower lakes or shores for crustaceans and shellfish.

THE PLUMED SERPENT

Quetzalcoatlus is named after Quetzalcoatl, the mythical plumed serpent worshipped by the ancient peoples of Mexico such as the Toltecs and Aztecs. Even though Quetzalcoatlus wasn't feathered, its slender jaws, long neck, head crest and size would have given it an awesome appearance – even compared with the powerful dinosaurs of the time.

Quetzalcoatlus may even have preyed on small or baby dinosaurs. An injured dinosaur would have been a lucky find for such a colossal, hungry creature.

TRANSATLANTIC FLYER

Quetzalcoatlus was lightweight, with a skeleton of hollow bones, and it had no heavy teeth, yet it had massive wings. This meant it could travel greater distances, non-stop, than a passenger plane can today. Rising on warm air currents and gliding on breezes, it hardly needed to flap its wings. To find food, it could fly at speeds of 130 kph (80 mph) and for distances as great as 19,300 km (12,000 miles) – that's almost halfway around the world!

QUETZALCOATLUS VERSUS MICROLIGHT AIRCRAFT

	QUETZALCOATLUS	MICROLIGHT AIRCRAFT
WINGSPAN	11 m / 36 ft	9 m / 30 ft
WEIGHT	100 kg / 220 lb	300 kg / 661 lb
SPEED	130 kph / 80 mph	250 kph / 156 mph

CRESTED COMPETITORS

Nyctosaurus (NICK-toe-SORE-us) had one of the longest head crests of all the pterosaurs. The bony, L-shaped growth was massive, with a length of 0.5 m (1 ft 7 in) – four times longer than its skull.

These mighty adornments may have been used to scare off other pterosaurs that were competing for the best feeding grounds. Just as stags use their antlers in fights during the mating season, the male Nyctosaurus may have used its crest to wage midair battles, swinging it like a sword as it wheeled through the air.

MISSING CLAWS
Mysteriously, there were no claws on the second, third and fourth fingers of Nyctosaurus's hands. Without these, it wouldn't have been able to cling to cliffs or trees, so probably spent most of its time patrolling the air.

SOARING EXPERT
The shape of Nyctosaurus's body and wings suggest that it was a top flier, able to turn sharply and capture air currents that would increase its speed as it soared.

FISH SKEWERS
The beak was long and sharply pointed to help it skewer fish as it dipped into the sea.

MINI FLYER

The small pterosaur, Tapejara (TOP-ay-HAR-ah), had a crest formed from two bones with a flap of skin stretched between them. This was probably for display more than flight. It flew for short periods throughout the day and night, snapping up fish with its beak. The short, downturned beak was strong, and some scientists think its shape was adapted for eating fruit, not fish, while others think it may have been used to tear at the flesh of carcasses.

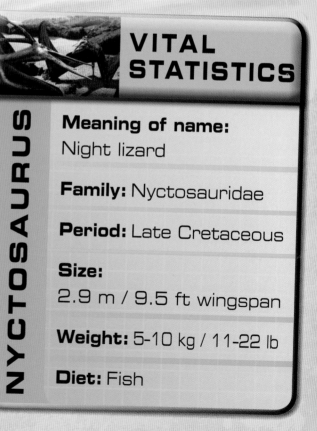

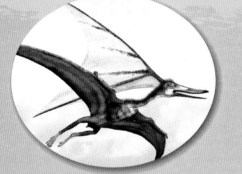

SKIN SAIL

Although there is as yet no evidence from fossils, some experts have suggested that a skin attachment may have stretched across Nyctosaurus's crest like a sail. This could have been for display, or to help with aerodynamics. With a twist of the head a sail crest could have caught a breeze or air current, allowing for fast changes of direction in mid-air.

VITAL STATISTICS

NYCTOSAURUS

Meaning of name:
Night lizard

Family: Nyctosauridae

Period: Late Cretaceous

Size:
2.9 m / 9.5 ft wingspan

Weight: 5-10 kg / 11-22 lb

Diet: Fish

KEEN-EYED KILLERS

To catch fast-moving fish, pterosaurs had to have sharp eyes and brains that could respond quickly, so they could home in on their kill. Anhanguera (ahn-han-GAIR-ah) had a large brain, so it was able to keep an eye on a swimming target while co-ordinating its flight to grab it.

SILLY LEGS

When Anhanguera sat down it would have looked rather odd. Its little legs would have spread out on either side of its body – they weren't built to be tucked neatly underneath like a bird's.

OLD DEVIL

In the Cretaceous period, pterosaurs evolved some strange-looking features. Anhanguera, which means 'old devil', had crests at the far end of its top and bottom jaws. Its teeth were sharp and stuck out at the end, like a fishing net of bony spikes.

SENSITIVE WINGS

The wings sensed any air movements that might help or hinder its flight. Its brain controlled the position of the wings.

The fossilised skulls of pterosaurs give us information about the size and different parts of their brains. Large 'optic lobes' show that their eyesight was good; smaller 'olfactory lobes' suggest that pterosaurs did not have a strong sense of smell.

GIANT FLIER

Ornithocheirus (or-nith-oh-CARE-us) had a wingspan of about 5 m (16 ft), making it the largest flying reptile of the Middle Cretaceous. The crests on its beak had a semicircular shape and became narrower near the end. This may have helped it push its mouth through the water as it swam over the surface of the sea. Its teeth didn't stick out, so instead of a mouth like a fishing net, it had the weaponry to snap up larger fish.

BIRD-LIKE BITERS

The first bird-like creatures weren't like most of the birds we are familiar with today – they had vicious dinosaur-like equipment, such as clawed wings and sharp, pointed teeth. Archaeopteryx (are-kee-OP-ter-ix) is the oldest known such creature, and lived with the dinosaurs in Jurassic times.

Archaeopteryx had feathers similar to those of today's birds, enabling it to fly. The feathers would also have helped to insulate its body, keeping it warm and dry.

BRIGHT FEATHERS?

We know that some of Archaeopteryx's feathers were black, but like birds today they were probably brightly coloured for communication, for example to attract a mate. We know that other prehistoric bird-like creatures, such as Sinosauropteryx (SIGH-no-sore-OP-ter-ix), had patterned feathers, and Archaeopteryx probably did as well.

LONG FINGERS

Its front limbs had developed into wings, but it still had finger claws, just as dinosaurs like Troodon did. It could probably fold its wings to its chest and overlap its claws.

BITING TEETH

Archaeopteryx was the size of a raven. But unlike modern birds, it had sharp, pointed teeth for biting and tearing at its prey.

BIG FEET

Big feet and toes enabled Archaeopteryx to grasp onto branches if necessary, but it could also walk along the ground on its strong legs to search for food.

BONY TAIL

Archaeopteryx's tail was bony rather than being made just of feathers. Its body was heavy compared to modern birds, so it wouldn't have been a good flier. For these primitive birds, flight may have been like extended leaping, flying for short bursts before gliding down to the ground again.

EARLY BEAKS

Confuciusornis (con-FEW-shus-OR-nis) didn't have teeth – it was one of the earliest birds to have a beak. Its beak may have been sharp enough to give a vicious bite though, like a modern-day goose. It had the longest feathers, compared to its body, of all the known forerunners of birds. But the lack of a fan-shaped tail for flight probably meant that it wasn't an agile flier, especially at low speeds. Fossil remains show that its plumage had different colours, including red, brown and black.

 **FLYING MONSTER** DETECTIVES

Archaeopteryx was an important discovery because it helped to show how birds developed from dinosaurs. It was a missing link in the evolutionary chain, possessing features of the theropod dinosaurs (a bony tail and sharp teeth) and features of today's birds (feathers and a forked bone between the neck and breast).

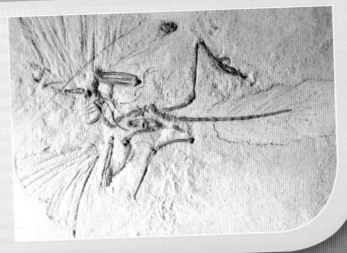

FLYING FAMILIES

Some pterosaurs may have flown solo, but it is likely that most flew together in groups, like modern-day birds. Small groups of three or four pterosaur fossils have been found together, while tens of pterosaurs of the same species have also been found together, suggesting a whole flock.

FROM A SAFE HEIGHT...

The remains of pterosaur nests have never been found, but many scientists believe that they would have built nests high on cliffs, like today's seabirds such as guillemots. There is evidence that Pteranodon built their nests in trees further inland. By nesting high up, pterosaurs and their hatchlings would have been safe from the killer dinosaurs. It is likely that they gathered in colonies, with a few males guarding a large group of females.

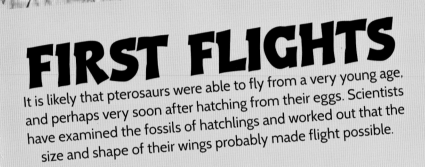

FIRST FLIGHTS

It is likely that pterosaurs were able to fly from a very young age, and perhaps very soon after hatching from their eggs. Scientists have examined the fossils of hatchlings and worked out that the size and shape of their wings probably made flight possible.

EGGS AND NESTS

On the basis of fossil evidence, pterosaurs' eggs appear to have had a very thin and leathery shell. To stop the eggs from drying out, pterosaurs would have had to bury them in a nest of vegetation or in the sand – just like the turtles' eggs shown below.

DINOSAUR DETECTIVES

In 2014, palaeontologists in China made an exciting discovery: fossilised pterosaur eggs that still had their original oval shape. The fossils of 40 Hamipterus (ham-IP-teh-russ) pterosaurs were found nearby, showing that the creatures had nested in a colony. They may have been wiped out by a storm. Analysis showed that the eggs were similar to snakes' eggs (shown here), with a thin, flexible shell.

WINGED WORLD

Pterosaur fossils have been discovered all around the world. This map shows a few examples.

NYCTOSAURUS

FOUND IN: *North America*
WHEN IT LIVED: *Late Cretaceous (85-65 million years ago)*
Fossils of several Nyctosaurus have been found in Kansas, USA.

QUETZALCOATLUS

FOUND IN: *North America*
WHEN IT LIVED: *Late Cretaceous (70-65 million years ago)*
Fossils of two Quetzalcoatlus have been found, in Texas, USA. The first fossil discovered was a part of a wing, found in 1971.

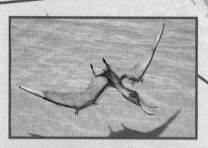

PTERODAUSTRO

FOUND IN: *South America*
WHEN IT LIVED: *Early Cretaceous (140-130 million years ago)*
The fossil remains of one filter-feeding Pterodaustro revealed that it used stones in its throat to help break down the hard outer covering of the creatures it ate.

Pterosaurs came in a huge variety of sizes. They ranged from the creatures as small as songbirds to the biggest flyer ever known, Quetzalcoatlus. Here they are shown with a modern golden eagle.

flying reptile wingspans
- ■ Dimorphodon – 1.8 m (5.9 ft)
- ■ Golden Eagle – 2 m (6.6 ft)
- ■ Nyctosaurus – 2.9 m (9.5 ft)
- ■ Pterodaustro – 3 m (9.8 ft)
- ■ Quetzalcoatlus – 11 m (36 ft)

DIMORPHODON

FOUND IN: Europe/North America
WHEN IT LIVED: Middle-late Jurassic (175-160 million years ago)
The first female palaeontologist, Mary Anning, found the remains of a Dimorphodon in 1828, in Dorset, England. They weren't correctly identified as a pterosaur until skulls were found in 1858. Dimorphodon fossils have also been found in the USA.

EUDIMORPHODON

FOUND IN: Europe
WHEN IT LIVED: Late Triassic (210 million years ago)
Eudimorphodon, one of the earliest known pterosaurs, was first discovered in 1973 in Italy.

RHAMPHORHYNCHUS

FOUND IN: Europe/Africa
WHEN IT LIVED:Late Jurassic (165-150 million years ago)
Many Rhamphorhynchus fossil bones have been found, along with some impressions of its wings.

ANHANGUERA

FOUND IN: Australia/South America/Europe
WHEN IT LIVED: Early Cretaceous (125-115 million years ago)
Anhanguera was first named in 1985, after fossils were found in Brazil. Since then it has been found in Australia and Europe.

TIMELINE
OF LIFE ON EARTH

Scientists have divided the billions of years of prehistoric time into periods. Dinosaurs lived in the Triassic, Cretaceous and Jurassic periods, while modern humans evolved in the Quaternary period.

← CAMBRIAN
541–485 mya: Life forms become more complex.

↓ SILURIAN
443–419 mya: First creatures on land.

↑ ORDOVICIAN
485–443 mya: Arthropods (creatures with exoskeletons) rule the seas. Plants colonis e the land.

↑ PRECAMBRIAN
4,570–541 million years ago (mya): The first life forms appear. They are tiny, one-celled creatures.

↑ DEVONIAN
419–359 mya: First insects evolve. Fish now dominate the seas.

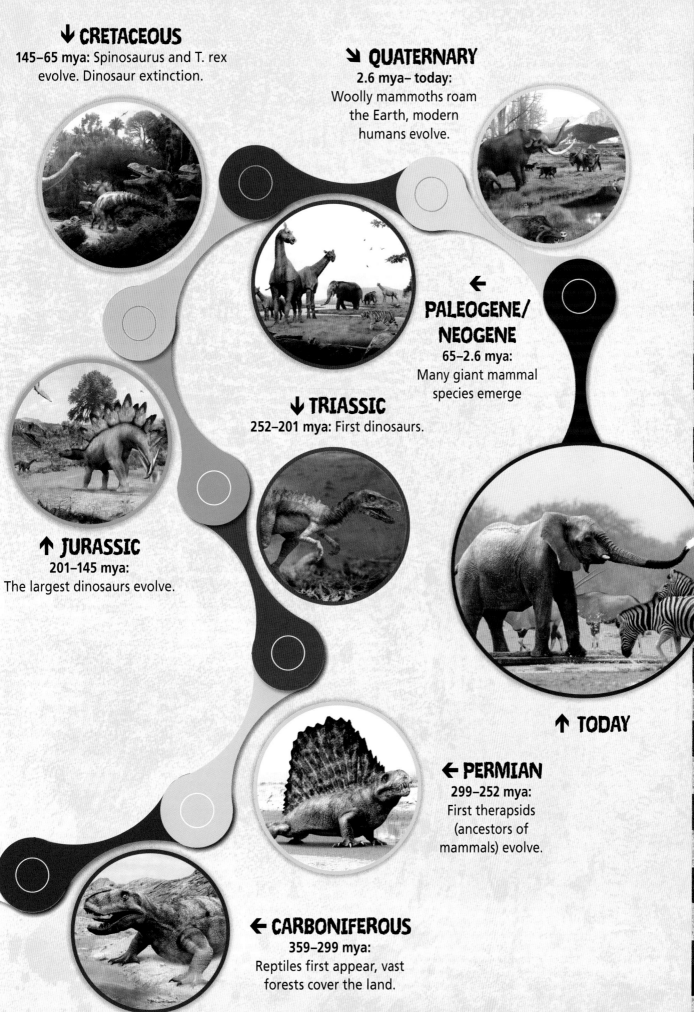

↓ CRETACEOUS
145–65 mya: Spinosaurus and T. rex evolve. Dinosaur extinction.

↘ QUATERNARY
2.6 mya– today: Woolly mammoths roam the Earth, modern humans evolve.

← PALEOGENE/ NEOGENE
65–2.6 mya: Many giant mammal species emerge

↓ TRIASSIC
252–201 mya: First dinosaurs.

↑ JURASSIC
201–145 mya: The largest dinosaurs evolve.

↑ TODAY

← PERMIAN
299–252 mya: First therapsids (ancestors of mammals) evolve.

← CARBONIFEROUS
359–299 mya: Reptiles first appear, vast forests cover the land.

GLOSSARY

breeding season Months in the year when creatures gather to mate in order to have offspring.

Carboniferous A prehistoric period when there were many swamps and forests. Fossil fuels later formed from the trees and plants that died.

carcass The body of a dead creature.

carrion Flesh from a creature that has died, and a source of food for some birds and animals.

Cretaceous A prehistoric period during which mammals and giant dinosaurs lived, and which ended with the mass extinction of the dinosaurs 65 million years ago.

Devonian A prehistoric period, also known as the Age of Fishes, when the oceans were warm and filled with many types of evolving fish.

evolve To change gradually over time.

extinct Not existing anymore.

filtering Extracting food, such as tiny fish from water, by passing it through sieve-like parts of the mouth.

flamingo A pink or reddish wading bird with long legs, a long neck, and a duck-like bill.

food chain A group of organisms arranged in order of rank, with each dependent on the next as a source of food. For example, a fox eats a mouse, the mouse eats an insect, and the insect eats a plant.

fossil The remains of a prehistoric organism preserved in rock.

fossilised Made into a fossil.

insulation A way of keeping heat in and cold out.

Jurassic A prehistoric period in which many large dinosaurs lived. It is also called the Age of Reptiles.

palaeontologist A scientist who studies fossil animals and plants.

predator An animal that hunts other animals to kill and eat.

prey An animal that is hunted by other animals for food.

pterosaurs A group of flying reptiles that were closely related to the dinosaurs.

reptiles Cold-blooded animals that usually lay eggs and have scales.

Triassic A prehistoric period during which the first dinosaurs and mammals evolved.

wingspan The measurement across the wings of an animal, such as a bird or a pterosaur, when the wings are outstretched.

FURTHER INFORMATION

FURTHER READING

Dinosaur Record Breakers by Darren Naish (Carlton Kids, 2014)

Dinosaurs: A Children's Encyclopedia by editors of DK (Dorling Kindersley, 2011)

Evolution Revolution by Robert Winston (Dorling Kindersley, 2009)

National Geographic Kids: The Ultimate Dinopedia by Don Lessem
(National Geographic Society, 2012)

Prehistoric Safari: Flying Monsters by Liz Miles (Franklin Watts, 2012)

The Usborne World Atlas of Dinosaurs by Susanna Davidson
(Usborne Publishing, 2013)

WEBSITES

http://www.bbc.co.uk/nature/14343366
A regularly updated part of the BBC website, dedicated to dinosaurs.
There is a news section and plenty of cool videos.

http://animals.nationalgeographic.com/animals/prehistoric/
This part of the National Geographic website is home to some fascinating
articles about dinosaurs. There are also some excellent pictures.

www.nhm.ac.uk/kids-only/index.html
The young people's section of the Natural History Museum website. Packed
with downloads, games, quizzes and lots of information about dinosaurs.

INDEX

SERIES CONTENTS

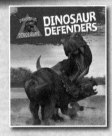

DINOSAUR DEFENDERS
Attack and Defence • Triceratops: Horn-Faced Fighter • Frightening Frills • Pachycephalosaurids: Butting Boneheads • Stegosaurus: Savage Spiker • Ankylosaurs: Defensive Demons • Hadrosaurs: Deafening Duckbills • Sauropods: Tail-Thrashing Titans • Patterns and Feathers • Herding Heavies • Danger Senses • Dino World • Timeline of Life on Earth

DINOSAUR RECORD-BREAKERS
Battling Giants • Titanosaurs: The Heavyweights • Smallest Dinosaurs • Ultimate Hunter: Spinosaurus • Deadliest Dinosaur • Skyscrapers • Dinosaur Egg Records • Fastest Dinosaurs • Longest Claws • Tough as Tanks: Best Protection • Smart Cookies or Bird Brains? • Famous Fossils • Timeline of Life on Earth

DINOSAURS AND THE PREHISTORIC WORLD
Dinosaur Planet • Changing Earth • Timeline of Life on Earth • Underwater Creatures • Emerging onto the Land • Early Reptiles: Fierce Forerunners • The First Dinosaurs: Hungry Hunters • Age of the Dinosaurs • Dino Diets • Extinction Event • After the Dinosaurs: Savage Mammals • Descendants of the Dinosaurs • Dino World

KILLER DINOSAURS
Ultimate Predators • Tyrant Lizard • Ravenous Giant • Utahraptor: Vicious Pack Hunter • Sickle-Clawed Runners • Carnotaurus: 'Flesh-Eating Bull' • Troodon: Night Tracker • Terrifying Teeth • Baryonyx: Fish Hunter • Packs and Families • Savage Killers or Just Scavengers? • Dino World • Timeline of Life on Earth

FLYING MONSTERS
Savage Skies • Needle-Toothed Terrors • Pteranodons: Awesome Axe-Heads • Jutting-Jawed Pterosaurs • Dimorphodon: Tooth-Beaked Hunter • Furry Fiends • Quetzalcoatlus: Giant Vulture • Crested Competitors • Keen Eyed Killers • Bird-Like Biters • Flying Families • Winged World • Timeline of Life on Earth

SEA MONSTERS
From the Deep • Shell Shock • Cameroceras: Tentacled Terror • Super-Sharks • Long-Necked Hunters • Liopleurodon: Jurassic Tyrant • Massive-Jawed Monsters • Ichthyosaurs: Fish-Lizards • Fearsome Fish • Giant Crocs • Changing Seas • Fossil Finds • Timeline of Life on Earth